# Cracks in the Dark

*Poems*
*by*

*Beverly C. Finney*

*Redhawk Publication*
*Catawba Valley Community College Press*
*2550 US Hwy 70 SE*
*Hickory NC 28601*



*ISBN: 978-1952485-48-0*

*Library of Congress Number: 2021951608*

*Second Edition*

Praise for ***Cracks in the Dark...***

*In the art world artists often say that one aspect of the process of making a painting is the joy of the "long look" they hope viewers will take as they linger in front of the piece.*

*Beverly's work comes from taking a long look at day-to-day circumstances and describing them physically and emotionally. She incorporates mindfulness, the ability to observe the environment in a non-judgmental way and acknowledge that it is all you have at the moment. Her work evokes a visceral response and, often for me, a sense that I have experienced something similar. That response is one of hope, joy and the familiarity and universality of the human experience.*

–John Worm, The Counseling Group

*Beverly Finney's poetry is a window to every soul. Her images illuminate the positivity of the world shrinking in darkness. Her messages of hope are contagious. Like me, you will probably gift this book year after year.*

—Evelyn Asher, author of poetry collections *What She Carries;* and *A Gypsy's Tapestry. A Woman Observed. A Woman Observing.*

Cracks in the Dark *leads us from watching our lives from the circumference to experiencing our moments from the center. Beverly Finney writes with unabashed honesty, vulnerability and courage, and brings to us the gift of presence with an open heart. Her soulful pouring compels us to slow down— to see, to hear, to share, to be —lest we miss the awe of the moment right in front of us that begins to turn the darkness into light.*

—Julie C. Fleck, therapist and life coach

*I have savored Beverly Finney's poetic exploration of how the light can reach us in these times of turmoil that seem daily to become ever more frantic, frightening, painful and intrusive.* Cracks in the Dark *invites us to slow down, take some deep breaths and savor just a few of these poems at a time. They may help you feel calmer, to look inwardly and outwardly more deeply. They are a joy to me and can be read and re-read for more depth and beauty with each reading. Raised in a large Welsh farming family myself, I especially treasure the poems in the last section, remembering cow paths leading to the creek, feeling the summer heat of the red clay of Beverly's home place, tasting luscious fig preserves on warm biscuits and catching vivid glimpses of those hard-working, loving people who raised her in Catawba County, NC.*

—Mary Perkins, *writer, storyteller and author of one volume of poems, Turning Toward Home, published in the United Kingdom. Also six other titles on the history and teachings of the Bahá'í Faith. Some of her work has been translated into fifteen languages.*

*Ring the bells that still can ring*
*Forget your perfect offering*
*There is a crack, a crack in everything*
*That's how the light gets in.*

–Leonard Cohen, "Anthem" from *The Future*

# *Foreword*

The poems in this collection have been written over a decade in my search for *being*, one moment, one thought, one poem at a time. In a way, they seem all over the map, but in their essence, they are part of my exploration to understand more fully what it means to be human. I offer them to you in a time it seems we need to consider our reason for being and our place in community with others.

I share them as prompts of sorts to your own search for bits of light in times of turmoil, division and uncertainty. They are there if we pay attention, are open to them: sharp slivers of awareness, dappled shadows of reflection, faint glows in warm hues of memory, flecks of joy like gold dust in the sifting pan. Sometimes, we simply must accept the dark, but hope lies in the cracks. There, we remember why we go on.

Always, a ton of gratitude to my supportive friends and family, especially the extra-miles of support of my husband Michael. And to my publisher Robert Canipe at Redhawk Publications, who, bless his bones, believes in me, as well as Tim Peeler who read and offered sound suggestions for the manuscript. I am also especially grateful to John Worm, a community "helper" who graciously read these poems in light of those who seek his guidance in troubling times and gave me generous and encouraging feedback.

---

Note: *I Come from Fig Preserves* first published in *Kakalak 2015*
*Old Comforts* first appeared on *YourDailyPoem.com 2019*
*Snapshots of Country Summers* first published in *Wild Goose Review, 2017*

## *Invitation*

Even if you are wont, as I am, to carefully turn pages, protect spines and covers and leave a book as unsullied as you found it, I invite you to treat this one as a workbook, a journal.

In addition to the pages provided for your own thoughts, I hope you will underline, highlight, turn down corners, make notes in the margins where a poem might light a spark in you.

Or take exception to the poem, offer a counterpoint, share how your experience differs. Stuff between the pages your own poem in response, or one by a favorite poet.

I offer this collection to inspire you to keep on. Live with it as you read, as if you were in conversation with a friend. You do not have to be a poet or a writer, only someone willing to engage in seeking light. And if you wish, I invite you to drop me a note at finneystudio@gmail.com.

Scan this code with a smartphone or other device to send Beverly an e-mail!

# Table of Contents

*Seek*

*Remember*

## *Borrow*

*In days of darkness*

*I survive on light borrowed*

*from other flames.*

## Last Thursday

Spotting a broken stem of oriental cherry,
on a whim I carry it
to two lovers holding each other
on a bench in the park.
*I found this, think it is yours,*
my romantic gesture.
Her face upturns to see the pink blooms
as tears so close spill
from the woman's eyes, not for me
or the pink petals or her companion.
What else now but to sit beside her, wait
for some sign, a voice of guidance,
the divine intervention of some providence.
She falls into my arms, sobs as I hold her.
*You talk to her,* her companion says, slipping away.
She talks to me, tells me her story.
I listen, choose what I say
with compassion, hoping she will
know I understand enough.
*It's already better,* she says finally, gently smiling.
*You gave me something, I will give you a song.*
She sings to me a song that comes pure
from her soul as if no one
were listening but God.
It is a prayer for both of us.

## Rose and Lattice

*for Pam and Eric on their wedding day*

Like a climbing rose, she weaves
herself in, out and through,
blooms unfolding as she goes.

Like the lattice where she grows,
he stands firmly grounded,
opening himself to her ascent.

Without her, he would be modestly
useful, an architectural appendage
in need of a meaningful purpose.

Without him, she would bunch,
sprawl, bloom still, but never
with the radiance of her promise.

Through the seasons, she will need
trimming and care; he will require
repair and occasional reinforcement.

And with that, she will keep blooming,
winding in and through his steadfast
presence where they are entwined.

## Solace of Small Things

The first green shoots
of daffodils in mid-winter,
the redbird on the bare branch
outside my window,
the warmth of the sun
on a brisk windy day,
the brown eyes of my pup
longing into my blues,
the full-throated song
of the mockingbird,
the comfort of a cup
of coffee in the morning,
the taste of strawberries,
the smell of baking bread,
the touch of my beloved's hand
just before falling asleep.

## Observations

Three years hence I tell him
how he tenderly lifted me
from a bitter berth of despair.
I share my embarrassing
bump-up moments afterward
in the crowded parking lot,
my mind still swirling euphoric
with our erstwhile encounter.

We laugh, he apologizes
for his part in my mishap,
thanks me for sharing
this passing engagement
set up in my memory
like a marker of stone.
*You are kind to tell me*,
he smiles over the counter.

I think of the anonymous
souls who hear our stories,
unwittingly give comfort
while ringing up goods,
making change and small talk.
Do they know it is a gift?
This one, quietly pleasant,
seems innately generous.

Only later, I, for the first time,
see him out in the aisle, twisted
legs impeding his labored efforts.
Now I know why he always
sits at his post, how bravely
he lives with humble gratitude.
Another stone set in memory.
I will not tell him about this one.
It goes beyond any words.

## A Small Miracle on Christmas Eve

Her brown toboggan with its lose threads
is pulled down over her forehead
as she cautiously watches the cashier
ring up her order of groceries.

She looks at the digital screen,
then quietly tells the cashier
to put some of the things back ...
flour, butter, half a dozen staple items.

I try not to read into her face
what might not be there, maybe shyness,
perhaps a moment's hesitation, a quiet
resignation she'd come up short.

Without deciding, I sidle past the line
to get the cashier's attention until she turns
to look at me: R*ing up the rest, I'll scotch*
I try to say without commotion or drama.

Without drama, she accepts the cash
the woman slowly draws from an envelope,
counts it out, turns to me across the aisle.
*Nine more dollars*, she says.

The woman in the brown toboggan offers
a soft thank you as she directs her cart
toward the door into the brisk December
air of this Christmas Eve.

*You're welcome. Merry Christmas,* I return
casually, barely making eye contact.
I gather up my goods without drama,
both of us go home to our loved ones.

What I want, though, is to throw my arms
around this sister in distress, tell her
it is she who has gifted me in my need
for the joy of being present in this season.

## Rehab for the Visiting

Though he lies sleeping in his small bed,
his back to her and the window facing south,
his wan face shadowed in his bent frame,

she sits quietly beside him watching the rise
and fall of his body, thinks about his infirmity,
his strength and persistence, the calamities

of an indiscriminate fate, how he still smiles
warmly, quips with humor and is luminous
in the presence of those loving and loved.

In the stillness of the late afternoon, as light
echoes tinkle and thump down the long hallway,
she closes her eyes against the rigors of her day,

of her life, ignores the urging of her Citizen's
watch to hurry home to her hungry family.
Here, in this place of ruin and inevitable

departure, in the soft breeze of the window
now open to life's end, the precious worn silks
of fading spirits gently billow, threadbare

but still lovely with kindness, courage
and amusement, gently lifting in small joys.
That he is unaware of her presence only

serves the real purpose of her visits here.
She has come for herself, to be reminded
of what matters most at the end of anything.

## Decision

Maybe hope is a choice
she says to her father
seeking advice on starting
a family when the future
seems so uncertain,
if not determinedly bleak.
Children are expressions
of hope, he offers,
as you were to me
in my own tremulous times.
Hope takes our hand,
shines light on our path,
welcomes us into the house
of living fully human.
Her father, seeker of stars,
scholar of the heavens,
must surely be wise.
She will give her child
her father's name.

## Finally, a Little Reparation

Sisters, close since birth, move up north
together, live together, bear children
together, take turns cooking, cleaning
and looking out for each other.

> *City fathers, in time, build a highway*
> *through that neighborhood to separate*
> *themselves from the Blacks, then just stand*
> *by while everything across that road crumbles*
> *into dereliction right down to the sewer pipes.*
> *So the sisters, all their neighbors have to move*
> *out while they sue the city for its gross neglect.*

Somehow, the sisters are separated.

> *Forty years the city fights the judge's ruling*
> *for the plaintiffs until someone decent*
> *finally says, ENOUGH!*
> *Then sets about finding homes for the few*
> *who can be found still living*

Forty years the sisters live lost to one another.
One sister, then quickly found, the other
elusive, unconvinced she should come forth
unless they find her a place close enough
the two sisters can wheel their chairs no more
than a block or two to visit once again.

They do one better: a house next door
where the sisters chat over their phones,
looking into the other's window, waving.

Why did she hesitate, they ask her later,
and she sighs: *When you lose your home,*
*lose your family and then your health,*
*how you gonna feel good about yourself?*
*You give up. You just don't care no more.*

Is she happy how it all turned out?
*Oh, yes,* she sighs again, and then a tender
whisper, *'cause I finally got my sister back.*
After all this time it is not a lot to ask,
but for her and her sister, it is enough.

## Found

*after* A Pilgrim's Song *by Vickie Jo Franks*

What of those who live *found* lives,
cobbled together from the scraps and refuse
discarded by those who have too much,
piecing a bare-knuckles tapestry of survival?

Intrepid scavengers with eyes that see
in a different light, creative imaginations
full of new visions for what's tossed aside,
clever hands, forging hearts fashioning anew.

How rich are they in fierce attention
to the overlooked, in the satisfaction
of self-sufficiency, the prayer of gratitude,
the tiny fragments of beauty, hope and joy?

# Just One Wish

Little Shaver, maybe five, his dark
hair cut close to his head, his small hand
tugging on the hem of Big Guy's shorts.
*Big* as in two hundred forty pounds
of linebacker, hard and mean, NFL bound.

One of a dozen youngsters on a generous
spree to encourage them to play sports,
wiggles milling around, giddy in their fortune
and the company of the soon-to-be gridiron star
corralling them into choices undreamed of.

Enough money to purchase a full outfit—
cleats, uniform, helmet—double their daddies'
weekly pay at the going minimum wage,
enough to buy a month's groceries for four,
a *google-eyed-more-green-than-I've-ever-seen.*

All theirs to grant extravagant wishes,
Christmas come early among rows, racks,
tables and shelves of *what-do-you-want-buy-me*!
But Little Shaver is focused on one wish,
one heart's desire burning hot inside him.

*Can we find this boy a football?* Big Guy asks.
Little Shaver looks up, way up, small brown fingers
of one hand still clutching the hem of those shorts,
the other one rubbing his dark expectant eyes
trying to hold back, maybe even hide, the tears.

# Another Language

Distress shrieks from that boy
in his native dress who stands
nearly frozen in the narrow aisle,

tears streaming like hard rain
on the streaked window
of his small, terrified face.

On and on the wailing continues,
grows louder, more intense.
His mother cannot console him.

He has no language to explain,
no language even to connect
or from which to accept comfort.

She hesitates, the quiet woman
who would suffer patiently in silence
before complaining, who finds

her own comfort in anonymity,
even invisibility if it were possible.
It has always been her nature.

Somehow, she understands this boy,
hears his special need in his howling,
reaches for his hot trembling hand,

draws him to her, feels his distress release,
then sits hours with him in the aisle
drawing on the paper bags provided

for distressed stomachs on long flights.
Crooning, speaking reassurance
in intuitive soft smiling tones,

she melts his fears, coaxes a smile
from his upturned face, hears the rich
peal of his laughter, her own heart sing.

## Gratitude

The boy, eight years old,
with a dislocated knee
and burns from the waist down
tended by a foreign
doctor who becomes
his friend.

The father traveling far over
bombed out rutted roads,
to bring his son home healed,
his gift of gratitude, a mango,
warm and gently bruised
with the print
of his right thumb.

## What I Love

She told me love is for people
when I said I loved grapes
as she held them under
the faucet's running water.
But I still love cornbread
hot from the oven, crumbled
in a bowl, soaked in milk.
I love the compassion bell
on the bookshelf, the purity
of its reverberation lingering
under my skin like memory.
I love the books beside it,
and those shelved and stacked
in every possible space,
steadfast old companions.
I love the morning light
through the sunporch window
where I sip my coffee, read
and think of other things
I'm not supposed to love

... but I do.

## This Moment

On a rainy Wednesday morning
in September, I'm reading
the news over my first cup of coffee.
Just the two of us, resting
in the warmth of that green lamp
my daughter hates, where I tease
I will have my ashes interred.
I sit reading, pup curls into a ball
of warm fur—soft as any rabbit's—
on the back of the sofa, her white
plume of a tail brushing my arm.
Her breath is heavy with sleep,
mine somewhat irregular
as I realize I've been holding it
sometimes, but don't know why.
The street is quiet this morning,
a lull in the comings and goings.
I set my cup aside, lean my head
against her firm rump and breathe.
This is life in the moment.

## And Then She Sang

Into a dark land where rivers have run red
and the earth sprouted white crops of bones;

where the wild flash of machetes has silenced
a mountain of old men and babies;

where forsaken women, swollen with seeds
of great madness, have gathered their poor fruits
under a tree, around battered pans over frugal fires;

where any trace of hope survives only by one
thin, ragged strand, and some have long since gone
missing in jungles of horror, deserts of grief;

where day goes to night to day for exhausted travelers
on a wearisome journey with no destination,

comes a lone prophet patiently sowing new seed,
praying to exchange the occasional sweet sip of charity
for the bountiful bread of sustainable empowerment,

beginning with little more than the making
of brightly colored beads.

Now in the land, an oasis of sturdy brick huts
under dazzling tin roofs, where women, re-couraged,
are filling the bellies of blameless children,

sending them off to school each morning,
waving goodbye as they skip down the path.

Now, radiantly fresh with dreams they can believe,
women knead a life with their durable hands
from paper beads and small plots of land.

Sitting in her very own chair, under the roof
of her own brick house, the slender woman
with velvet ebony skin and a smile of pearls

recalls wondering what she would do the first
hours finally inside her impossible dream:
*I thought maybe I would sing all night.*

## Silver Moments in Iron Rust Times

*after reading* A White Turtle Under a Waterfall
*by Wang Wei (701-761 AD)*

The daily headlines give me the blues
grinding out what is wrong with our times.
Darkness of division, the plaintive grief,

the frothing foment of fear,
the insistence on *me* and *mine*
chafe like a shirt of coarse hair.

Sometimes we must simply turn away.
If there is any silver lining, it is that
held moments become precious.

The pink in the clouds reflecting
the sunrise in the patch of blue
outside my kitchen window.

The taste of fresh strawberries
and cream with morning oatmeal.
The soft rise and fall of my pup

draped in a deep doggie sleep.
The sound of water sliding silken
over glistening rocks in a cold stream.

The cheer in a voice on the phone
so delighted to hear my voice, too.
The smile of patience and respect

spontaneously offered by a stranger.
The words of a Chinese poem
written in the eighth century,

carrying a moment of beauty for all time:
*No angling or net fishing.*
*The white turtle lives out its life, naturally.*

# Be Gone

*for Naomi Faw*

*I know if I get into my art, I'll be gone. — Naomi*

Let's go in until we are gone.
Give over to our lusts
for creation, color,
textures and tubes,
the tactile of brush,
pallet, scissors, paper,
bright ribbons and glue.
Let's throw off cautions,
leave *should* and *ought*,
to tumble down that hole
where anything goes
as long as it takes us with it,
deep, deeper into gone.
Everything else can wait.
For joy, oh, joy, let us be gone!

## Corner Chair

Soft plump arms reach out,
an invitation to climb
into the wide lap,
soft and plump, too,
a grandmother of comfort
in a worn block-print dress
under the velvet light
of the squat lamp, the mist
of its beneficent glow warm
enough to induce sleep.
I curl up to dream.

*My borrowed light …*

## *Reflect*

*I am startled to find*

*there is light within when*

*I dare part the shades*

*of my own soul.*

## Dilemma of Conscience

*I know a man has all kinds of guns,*
*probably more than the law allows.*
*He shoots cans—Mexi-cans, Afri-cans,*
*Puerto Ri-cans,* he laughs.

The Mexicans come here, unskilled,
underbid his work, he says, then do
a half-assed job. He complains
to the contractors who hire them.

Cocksure, he is, that the Klan has
some good ideas though he doesn't
much agree with their violence.
His granddaddy was a Klansman.

He is plying his trade on my turf,
espousing his beliefs in a constant
chatter as he goes rhythmically
about his work, smoothing, assessing.

I admire his skill, his work ethic,
his bent to overcommit because
he can't say no when he is needed,
the stories that expose a big heart.

But this banter is wrong-headed,
at fierce odds with my own beliefs.
I know I should say something,
should speak up for what is right.

I am silent, tortured by my hesitation.
How to question his thinking
without dismissing the person,

this man of contradictions?

In the end, I let it pass unchallenged.
He will finish his work, get his pay,
move on to banter somewhere else.
I know silence is why nothing changes.

## Your Rights

You have the right to remain silent,
but should you when so much is at stake?

You have the right to remain ignorant,
but you cannot avoid the consequences.

You have a right to your opinion,
and earn respect when it's informed.

You have the right to indifference,
though you risk hardening of the heart.

You have the right to hate,
but prepare to be its object.

You have the right to be stupid,
though it requires accountability.

You have the right to look away,
but you will carry the ghost of shame.

You have the right to be wrong,
the opportunity to admit it.

You have the right to make mistakes,
to learn and grow from them, too.

So many choices you have
at every fork in your life's road.

What do you want them to say
at the end about who you were?

## Inventing the Devil

Burdened
by my own evil,
I invented the devil:
the color of my scarlet
anger, the horns of greed
and envy, the barbed tail
of vengeance, sharp hooves
of destruction, the giddy glee
of malice and deception.
I housed him in the fire
of my troubled soul,
hoping he would take
the heat of my iniquity,
conveniently absolve me
of my wrongdoing.

## Accepting the Truth

You don't have to be a Buddhist
to hold the belief that life
        is suffering,
though it might help to accept
the truth in that tenet
with more tolerance.

What is, well, simply is.

We wish it otherwise,
greedy for peace
and contentment
to shine on our days.

We do try to influence
the outcome with our
careful plans, prayers
for intervention and miracles,
and good hard work,
even succeeding a little.

In the end, however, life
        will be what it is.

We decide if it will break us.

## What If? Point:

What if it isn't your wiring
that's making your life such a mess?
What if it isn't your genes
that won't give your mind any rest?

What if it isn't the world
that just won't give you a break,
or won't give you the absolute cure
for all that makes your heart ache?

What if it's not others' desires
keeping you in such a state?
Or if it isn't destiny's devious plan
that's actually setting your fate?

What if all the right answers
don't come just in *either* and *or*,
or if there aren't any *right* answers
behind some magical door?

What if life just never will offer
a divine sweet fairytale ending,
no obviously perfect solutions
to set all of your problems mending?

What if this is all there is,
all that blows in the wind?
What if this is as good as it gets?
What do you think you will do then?

## What If? Counterpoint:

And what if it *is* your wiring or genes
that's driving you so to distraction?
What if it's something you cannot control
that's stoking your every reaction?

What if you can't firmly will it away
or talk it out of your system?
What if you're held strong in its grip
unless you take that prescription?

What if you're simply ordained to be
other than you might desire,
whipped excessively to and fro
by some wind or storm or some fire?

What if this state is your lot,
your handicap, if you so please,
the thing you decide you will live with
or let force you onto your knees?

So what if this is the way it is,
the course your life must now plot?
What if this is the hand you are dealt?
What'll you do with just what you've got?

## 10 Reflections on Leaning in on White Water

-1-

When the boat dips
wildly in riots of water
over the river's rocks,
lean in to stay afloat.

-2-

Sorrow peels the skin of hope,
slackens the muscle of resolve,
brittles the bones of courage.
Lean quietly into calm waters
eyes resting ...
pulse slowed ...
body extended ...
breath moving
with gentle rhythm
in and out ...
renew and ready for rapids ahead.

-3-

You may not journey
as you dreamed
in the usual vessel
down a well-charted
stream, but you can travel
in another, uniquely your own,
cast off from your untrammeled
shore, and then lean in
for a ride beyond any
those dreams could imagine.

-4-

Leaving behind what
has been loved pulls up
anchors of umber grief
and mossy deep longings.
Leaning into the current
carries you forward, inviting
ripples of luminous visions,
of wonder and discovery.

-5-

In the race of the rapids
we are prone to panic
just when we should
lean into paddling.
Not that we can control
our destiny, but to stay
engaged in the journey.

-6-

I am afraid. You are afraid, too.
But if we lean into each other
on these waters, we will arrive
together wherever we are.

-7-

The river may be long, the passage
assaulted with perils and pain.
Still, we must lean into the murky
shadows, into the spurious secrets
beyond the unfurling bends,
declaring with full-throated song
our rousing resolve to hold on.

-8-

If I do not lean, with faith,
into waters I do not know,
I can only fall over into those
I cannot hold back anyway.

-9-

Lean into the day's stretch
of the river washed clean
in the sun, tenderly soothed
by shadows, the air brightly
quivering with the trill of birds,
the rasping croak of frogs,
the earth gloriously aflutter
in the graceful weaving dances
of wildflowers in sweet grasses,
the flash of silver fish and blue heron.

-10-

Dare fear to drag you into the whirlpool
of despair, then defy him, letting go
of everything, rising again, buoyed
with rapture into the clean break of day
and deep draughts of lavender air.

## Something to Lose

I've always had something to lose.
And could afford to.
Good genes, productive people,
a roof, full belly and dreams.
More than needed.
*Want* was extravagance,
desire beyond survival,
not deprivation.

Born under a generous star,
can I know the want of hunger,
shabby shame of poverty,
futility of dreams, the emptiness?
How can I write of desperation
with authenticity and heart
if I always have something to lose,
and can afford to?

## Decluttering

Regrets piled in the dark corner,
permanently stained with neglect
or tattered from over wear, should
have been discarded long ago.
Why do I hang on to them unless
it's hoping I'll find a use for them yet?

Passions I've loved that once fit me
almost perfectly, brought out my best,
still with so much good purpose left in them.
But I'm on a new path, the time now
to pass them along to someone eager
for the joy of giving them a new life.

Good intentions I'm not quite ready
to give away or give up on,
thinking with a little alteration
here or there, a tuck or a few stitches,
a fresh touch, they could be revived,
once again suited for the right occasion.

I debate a couple of enduring dreams
I've cherished but rarely taken out,
reticent to risk soiling them with failure
or finding them one day worn too thin
with no replacement. What good are dreams
if they're only going to hold a place?

And here a gaggle of memories
I'll keep awhile yet for sentimental reasons,
some singular significance attached
that lends them a value beyond utility,
a few things to wrap myself in before
the mirror of time, see they are lovely still.

Stepping back, surveying the sort,
there's likely nothing I'll truly miss.
Letting go of the culls bagged for disposal
is cleansing, rewards me with a sense
of accomplishment and relief.
It is time, well past time, I know.

So, I ask, should I simply enjoy
the sense of order and freedom
that comes from purging?
Or might I indulge in something new
to give me a fresh way of seeing myself,
divine me to delightful discoveries?

Something smart, bolder, say,
with a snappy colorful appeal,
maybe a bit daring, or perhaps,
even totally out of character,
if the fit is right, the hue flattering,
my imagination fired up again?

## Believe

When I think to quit,
I remember the victories.
Tiny ones to be sure,
here and there,
but victories nonetheless.
If they do not shout praise,
they whisper assurance.
I would prefer fanfare,
of course. Wouldn't you?
Sometimes, however,
the truest things
come in a hushed voice
I can hear clearly enough
if I think to pay attention,
have the courage to believe.

## Just Know

Chaos is the natural
order of things.
To crave control
is to be paralyzed
in fear of making mistakes.
Ride the crest
of *what is,*
feel the curve
of *what is to be*
press you toward the shore.

## Exorcism

Paint heartaches in black, a thick coat
of darkness tangible enough
to fully expose them, unresolved.

Brush it on, then take to the pallet
knife to add texture, the swoops,
swirls and slashes of bitterness.

Persist until you feel the shadows
begin to drift out of your soul,
dappled light begin to filter in.

Breathe.

Breathe deeply.

Again.

Lay out the tubes of bright colors—
alizarin crimson, lemon yellow,
magenta, ultramarine blue.

Line all the brushes up in a row—
fans, rounds, filberts, angular, bright
and flat; clean the pallet knife.

Breathe. Again, deeply.

Then begin with a broad flat sweep
of lemon yellow, a fan of ultramarine,
until the canvas explodes with joy.

## From Afar I See More Clearly

*Love means to learn to look at yourself*
*The way one looks at distant things*
*For you are only one thing among many.*
—Czeslaw Milosz

As from a high outcropping near the peak above here,
I look down, see myself trying to make sense of the world,
to find my place in it, to wring the meaning out of living.
From this distance, I look like a pebble, a twig of an elm,
or maybe something like the feather of a small bird.

Whatever I am, it is clear
I am not the center of the universe.

I study my movements, up and down, this way and that,
labored then resting, moving again, never ranging far,
just clamoring over and under, in and out, like a beetle
or tiny blue lizard feeling my way to survival, unlike
them, impaired by the consciousness of my existence.

Whatever I am, it is clear
I toil, and with too much intention.

From here, I can see the futility of so much struggle,
the silliness of worry, the waste of doggedly searching
for what's been there all the time, available for the taking
in the small ebb and flow of my little days, hour after hour
of fulfilling my purpose and place by simply keeping on.

Whatever I am, it is clear
I am as I am, one thing among many.

## Answer to Why

Not because

I think I should
or feel I have to,
or someone asks
me to as a favor.

Not because

it is demanded,
or for the reason
it just seems to be
the right thing to do.

Not because

I am afraid not to,
or no one else offers
to do it, or will not
do it as well.

Not because

I think I will be
rewarded with fame,
fortune or even a cheap
rhinestone tiara.

But simply because I want to.

## Wonder

*In difficult times carry something*
*beautiful in your heart.* –Blaise Pascal

A place in you
that knows
no wounds,
pure, serene,
a sacred place
no one, no thing
can ever touch
or take away
from you.
Your heart
of hearts,
where beauty
blooms eternal,
beckoning you
to keep on.

## At the Heart of It

Dignity is what we crave.
To be treated as if we
are inherently worthy
simply in our existence.
Not because we have
wealth or status,
education or talent,
nor for the color of skin,
our language or faith.
Or even because we
can contribute something
of value to others.
None of these gets
to the heart of it,
the heart of our hearts.
No, it is to be inherently
worthy because we are.
Because we are.

## One-Degree Destiny

Only one small decision, one
momentary reaction, one unexpected turn

of events, one minor circumstance away
from who we become at last.

Something we decide to do
—or not;
something we take in
—or not;
something we let go of
—or not;
some way we respond
—or not;
some place we should have been
—or not ....

One degree this way or that defines our destiny.
One degree, just one degree, exponential in time.

## Distance

Distance in miles
is irrelevant
to love
who knows how
to read a map,
find alternate routes.
Distance in the heart
is the mileage
that constrains.
With no intent
to travel, the heart
has no need for a map.

*My reflections …*

## *Seek*

*Following the light of a single*

*flickering candle, I stumble*

*toward a path petaled*

*in luminous understanding*

## Seeking Self

-1-

That spirit which conceives
our dissatisfactions,
pushes our boundaries,
wears our cravings,
nudges our complacencies,
travels with us along the road
to understanding as we try
to make sense of our existence
is the restless worm
in our malleable brains,
forever burrowing,
churning the soil of *what if.*

-2-

To possess, to know, become,
achieve, arrive, move on.
To pacify, energize, resolve,
to liberate, define, emulate,
to cleanse, forgive, even the score.
To set boundaries, open doors,
shut out pain and deaden regret.
To step up, calm down, get through,
leave behind, carry on, start over.
Ever seeking, ever restless with what is,
ever wearing our discontent like an itch
in constant need of a good scratch.

## Quiet Time

*thinking of Wendell Berry's*
*Port William series*

When we were closer to the land,
daily wresting our lives and living
from the soil, wind, sun and rain,
work and meditation coexisted,
occurring simultaneously
in the quietly repetitive motions
of tilling, sowing and reaping,
in the rhythmic rotation
of the seasons where only
light and darkness mark time.

No devices connected us every minute
to anyone, everything in the world,
filling our hours, our heads
with a constant caffeinated buzz
—or its craving—of instant gratification.
With them we can know everything,
except who we are, what we believe,
where we hope our journey takes us.
For that, we need purpose, and the quiet.

## Same Sky

Over the salt marsh, the sky is a wash
of pinks, lavenders, a half dozen blues.

    Apricot, peach and mango brush the clouds,
spill full out where the sun is setting.

Sweet syrupy hues lie on the inlet
    between patches of saw grass and reeds fading
to silhouettes as day turns its page to evening.

It's the same over New York at this time of day,
later, Kansas City, Albuquerque, San Francisco.

    And the same over a park in a poor neighborhood
in India and behind the rude mud and thatch huts

of Zimbabwe, those same hues watercolor an identical
sky as it snuggles down into night.

Under this sky every human soul can look up, pause,
    aware of the closing of another day,
taking, for just a few moments, a breath of peace.

    How is it we share that sky, the same sun, moon
and this Earth yet be so far apart from each other?

## Where, Oh, Where?

Where, oh, where to find it,
the stoutness of heart
to go on in the dark
smoke of these times?
The world is on fire,
no haven offers safety.
We scatter in chaos,
regroup into tribes,
attack in fear, scramble
in dissonant desperation,
the blaze of kill or be killed,
all of us rightly claiming
to be victims. And we are,
of one ilk or another. Just ask us.
Where, oh, where to find it,
the way through to after
our near self-inflicted demise?
The world is on fire,
no havens offer safety.
How is it we find no shelter,
no solace in one another?

# Pandemic

A small spoon of the bitters
of living perpetually
with deprivation and death.
Can we imagine living
with war, its ravages
of starvation, disease
and deadly despair,
not for uncertain months,
but years, no end in sight,
no saviors, forgotten?
The same for the poor,
disabled, those living
daily hand-to-mouth
without dreams, much hope?
Can we imagine?
Now that we've tasted of it,
shouldn't we try?

## Goodness

What is the kernel
that sprouts in
those who bridge
where others choose
to divide, destroy?
Some small seed,
dormant perhaps,
that knows its time
to awaken, pushes
aside its old husk,
thrusts its roots
into the soil, lifts
its face to the sun
and rain, gives itself
up to posterity.

## Dismal Thinking

*for Susan Lahey*

*I do apologize for such dismal thinking — Susan*

Do not apologize for darkness.
It's part of the warp and weft
of your existence, of mine, too.
We shouldn't hide it, even,
and especially, in troubled times,
attempt to fake a sunny-side
up when we know that's a lie.
In it, we betray ourselves,
then others who conclude
they should follow our lead,
hide their anguish behind
plaster smiles, strangled cheer.
Not to wallow, but to invite
darkness in with care and respect.
It has come like a friend
to sit with us in our grief.

## Different Light

When the only light we can see
is the oncoming train barreling
down recklessly, we want to jump
in front of it, avert a disaster.
But if we turn aside, follow
the uplifted lantern to a circle
of illumined faces, eyes of hope,
the open arms of faith and trust,
how does the world look then,
in this different light?

## Blessing of Troubles

Not sky, but clouds
adding texture, shift-shaping
in the winds, forecasting,
reflecting morning sun
in hues of pink, lavender
and soft fuchsia.
Or curdling with cumulus,
swept with wisps and curls,
crisscrossed with contrails,
fresh and fading.
Without them, the sky
is a flat canvas in varying
shades of numbing
happily-ever-after.
How would we know
to celebrate the sun?

## Forgiving

I forgive you.
Here is my hand.
May I touch
your heart?
May I place
your hand
on my heart?
In the stillness
of our breath,
can you feel
the firm beat
of my desire
to come gently
to you even now,
especially now?
Will you accept
my gesture?
Will you sense
my simple ease,
my ready trust?
Can you trust
your forward step?
Will you meet me
here in the place
of new beginnings?

## Travel Advice

Because your best miles
are still ahead of you,
you must fuel up,
cull the baggage, take
a new route with nothing
more in mind
than the journey itself,
destinations of wonder,
engagement and reflection
to be discovered, not planned.

Along the way, sing forthrightly
your own version of *Song of Myself*,
make music to the distinct beat
of your soul's drum.
Walk joyously in the sun,
lift your face to the rain,
rest your back against an oak,
study the colors of the sky,
talk with the birds.

Invite worthy companions
to join you, share your bread.
Lend your staff if they falter
over rough ground, send them
on their way with the grist
of good humor,
the fragrant oils of gratitude,
the elixir of being alive,
alive, oh, alive!

## In the Absence of Perfection

Shall we not sing at all just
because we don't have perfect pitch?

Shall we never dare to love
because it holds the potential for pain?

Shall we make no promises,
afraid we might break one or two?

Shall we keep our dreams small
so they never disappoint?

Shall we not give in to pleasure
because deprivation feels safer than joy?

Shall we take no risk so we never
know the frustration of failure?

Shall we draw the circle so tightly
around our lives that we snuff them out?

## Hard Lessons

What do we learn
from salvation
in the nick of time?
Snatched from the teeth
of might-have-been,
momentarily relieved,
yes, even grateful.
But then, gone
into the hot wind
of moving on,
offering us false
faith in our luck.

It is salvation come
too late that saves us.
The gift of slogging through
the pain and grief
of what came to be
in the absence of safety.
It's falling over the edge,
missing the cue,
walking the hot coals
of the disaster that purifies us,
transforms complacency
into wonder and wisdom,
a gratitude that shimmers
even in our sleep.

## Insight

In that moment
when you know
what it's like to be
someone else,
that fragile moment
of fierce clarity
that cleanly opens
you to see the world
through his eyes,
feel it the way
her heart feels it,
dissolve into that skin
in a way you will
never forget,
cannot forget.
In that moment,
the ticking seconds
of insight clear
as spring water
at its source,
you are the best
you will ever be.

## Going Against the Grain

Promise to go against the grain
if your conscience is restless
with going along.

Promise to go against the grain
if someone without a voice
is getting lost in the din.

Promise to go against the grain
when compromising your principles
looks like the path of least resistance.

Promise to go against the grain
when life's road gets hard
and you are weary.

Promise to go against the grain
when someone doubts
your dreams or talents.

Promise to go against the grain
if taking care of yourself
begins to feel self-serving.

Promise to go against the grain
when you begin to doubt
that you are worthy.

Promise you will be true to yourself
so that you can be true to others, too.
Honor your promises, for they are holy.

## Words Are All We Have?

What of a melody, no lyrics,
just the notes, a story told
in a painting or photograph?
Think of how much the eyes
speak, how the body often signs
the truth in a simple shrug
or unconscious gesture of hands.
And what does it tell us when
someone shoulders in quietly
to help carry a cumbersome load?
What is conveyed in a touch
or a sigh, in a single sliding tear?
How much meaning in the spaces
between words, a long silence?

## What I Mean

What do I mean? Not
what I say means, but me?
Not just this scheme of bones,
tissue, nerves, this amalgamation
of billions upon trillions of cells,
but what inhabits this physicality
I live and move in, the thing whose
absence will make of me a corpse.
What do I mean, my place here,
how I fill it, what lives aside from my body?
This much I believe: I am my impact
here and now, every act a brush
stroke painting on the world
colors I may not see, textures
I do not intend in my heat and haste.
I am mistaken to think I am invisible,
of no consequence even if I wish it.
I mean something I search for,
pray it is something worthy
of the air I breathe, my space here.

## Seeking Truth

To find it you must avoid answers.
Search only for questions.

The best and truest,
the most worthy
have no answers.

Instead, they seize our minds,
lead us in passionate pursuit
of the nearly impossible.

Along this fearless journey
we begin to know ourselves
in ways frightening with clarity.

We begin to see the world
as it is, find our resolve to light
our small candle to dispel

what darkness we can
where we are, using what gifts
we have, until we have wrung

them out, worn, thin and dry.
There we may begin to find truth.

## Permission

*for Brittany Brown on turning 18*

You can be afraid
without drowning in fear.
You can have doubts
without feeling weak.
You can celebrate what
you've left behind
even in regretting
that it is over.
You can venture the new
without committing for life.
You can fail
without being a failure.
You can let go of what
you can't change
without giving up hope.
You can love deeply
without throwing yourself
under the train.
You can walk your own path
without leaving others behind.
You can leave others behind
without leaving them
out of your heart.

## What I Need to Know

I don't need to know
how much money you have
or how you got it;
how many degrees you have
or the fraternity or sorority
you claim; what kind of car
you drive, the square-footage
of your house, its address;
who you know, especially
if you deem them *important*.
What I want, yes, even need,
to know is what you believe
in your heart of hearts,
how your heart goes today,
who you love and the ways
you show it, what your spirit
longs for your hand cannot touch.

*My search …*

## *Remember*

*The light of memory casts*

*long shadows in the flame*

*of the torch from before,*

*asks me to carry it on.*

## Hankering

I have a hankering
to rediscover my roots.
Not the genealogy,
but the times, the land
my people came from,
made their lives on,
left behind long ago.
I yearn to walk the fields,
follow those paths,
breathe in the air
that still carries stories
of place, all the stories
over all time that inhabit
me, those I long to unfold
in sheaf by yellowed sheaf
of memories older than mine.

# I Come from Fig Preserves

I come from rich brown fig preserves,
with that coveted slice of candied
lemon rind and tiny seeds, spooned
liberally onto a warm buttered biscuit,
lifting the frost of a winter morning;

from the hefty plump fruits plucked
from the shadows of leaves, broken
open to a sumptuous pink pulp
that melts into a mellow sweetness
against the tongue in late summer;

from the warm southern exposure
of weathered barns and sheds
in whose shelter the fig bushes grew
and survived, offered cuttings handed
out and down for generations.

I come from real working farms,
from folks who rose before dawn
to make a living and a life right out
of the soil they turned and tended,
and from what the earth yielded;

from new potatoes, beans and tomatoes,
from spring onions, sweet fall turnips,
from persimmons and muscadines,
from damson plums and rusty coat
apples, from pecans and black walnuts.

I come from the soil in which they grew,
from the minerals left over from stardust,
from the rain and the sun and the cool
of nights, from the sweat of planting,
harvest and putting up for later.

I come from the bone of self-sufficiency,
the muscle in growing things, the skin
of bonding with the land, from hearts awake
to the splendid bounty of fig preserves
on a warm buttered biscuit in December.

## Hand-Me-Downs

Grandma's table sits in my kitchen,
somewhere around it the place my father ate,
a fresh-faced farm boy with earnest eyes
behind long dark lashes.

Grandmother's hand-penciled recipe
for watermelon rind preserves framed
on the wall nearby, script gentle like her,
my deepest experience in unconditional love.

My grandfather's worn bibbed overalls,
donated to my teen theatrics half a century hence
must find a place in my creative space, coaxing
from me his ingenuity and entrepreneurial spirit.

The jewelry chest my mother gave me years ago,
not useful for its purpose, always struggling for a niche,
still treasured as one of her last hand-chosen gifts
before cash seemed a more practical bequest.

Dad's shirts in his favorite colors, red and blue,
his soft worn jeans, await quilting to envelope me
in his enduring love and strength, reminding me
he said I'm made of the same courage and grace.

The little yellow nut chopper with its tiny handle,
a gift from a mother-in-law to dice pecans
for her son's favorite cake, surrendered only when
she conceded her baking days were over, a sign of trust.

Keepsakes, odd bits of my heritage,
connections to my roots finding their places,
grounding me in this season of my life
when I am passing my beloved keepsakes on.

## Barefoot

You can't grow up spending summers
going barefoot without filling your soles
and ten toes with a mash of memories.

Wet cool of early morning dew on the grass
you glide through in a dream of what you
might do with this day of free rein.

An aboriginal dance when you cross
the fiery hell-heat of pavement baking
in the hot Southern sun of late July.

Sharp sting of a bee if you carelessly wade
into a patch of white clover, pull the stinger,
foot quickly swelling into an aching stump.

Warm squish of a cow patty oozing up
like thick green pudding between your toes
as you gallop the path across the pasture.

Cutting edges of spent coal on the dirt road
to the barn when your grandfather cleans
the sooty cinders from his basement furnace.

Wading into the shallow creek behind that barn,
the one you drink from with the same disregard
you lick the salt block set out for the cows.

Pinch of patent shoes on Sunday morning
after a week of footsie freedom, complaints
of your toes praying for the benediction.

Up north, schoolteachers blame bare feet
for the sluggish intellect of Southerners,
skin exposed to soil, gateway for worms.

But down here we know how delicious it feels
to be part of the earth, to take in all this wonder
through the soles of our feet, our ten toes.

## Snapshots of Country Summers

... worn cow paths to the shallow creek,
sun-dappled shade of overhanging trees

... watermelon in the field, out of the rind, juice
on your face, dripping down your arms

... wooden bucket filled with ice and salt,
churning a freezing bowl of vanilla joy

... puddle knee-deep in a hay-field terrace,
a hard rain, heaven-sent wading hole

... blackberries on July Fourth, purple stains,
briar scratches, chigger bites—the price of jam

... barefoot through dust, mud, dew, scorching
pavement, the world through your feet

... June bugs, fireflies at dusk, bees in clover,
the buzz of crickets, the piping peep frogs

... corn on the cob, red ripe tomatoes, squash,
garden fresh with green beans, cucumbers

... windows open, sleeping in a drift of honeysuckle,
softly lowing cattle, dreams on silver moonbeams

# Half-Runner Sisterhood

Press the edge of the knife
against the stem, pull back
and feel the string unzip cleanly.
Repeat on the other end
against the soft thorn.
Then snap-snap, or maybe
snap-snap-snap if it's a long one.
It is not a chore to be over,
but a reverie of memories
around the tribal circle
of women's gossip and laughter
on the back porch in summer,
the rhythm of hands in a dance
of community and preservation
until the bushel basket is empty.
I sit alone on my porch now,
pan on my lap, half-runners
dripping onto yesterday's paper,
the edge of my knife unzipping,
the snap-snap familiar and sweet.
I am returned to the company
of those women who taught me
how to string beans, treasure secrets.

# Breakfast at Emolene's

Saturday morning in late summer,
skies sharply blue, the air cool
with just a whisper of a breeze,
the sun, warm, clean and bright.
We wind around mountain
roads to Independence, Virginia,
with Mom and George, accustomed
to breakfast well before this hour,
to fulfill our promise to sit at her table
in the hospitable 1843 farmhouse.

*Nobody makes biscuits as good*
*as Emolene's*, Mom declares.
I think she must be right
as I gently break open yet another,
brown and just a bit crusty outside,
soft, warm and light inside, served
hot and sometimes even buttered
from love and force of habit.
Platters of bacon, country ham
and sausage, bowls of scrambled eggs,
applesauce and rich brown gravy pass
from hand to hand, then generous
helpings of raspberry jelly, home-canned
fig and strawberry preserves.

We eat seconds, shameful thirds,
refilling our brightly colored coffee
cups as we listen to the obituaries
running on the local AM station.
We talk of death with relaxed
frankness, of those who may
somehow have deserved their
untimely ends, of the illnesses

and suffering of those
who surely deserved better,
of husbands and friends
gone, babies born and lost,
of the cruelties and blessings
that come of living a long life.
As she so often does these days,
Mom recalls her mother died
too young to see her children grown.

The tour has to be postponed
until we clear the kitchen table
so Emolene can lead us through,
delighting in our eager discoveries
among her collection of treasures.
One of them, an oaken dresser
her father made by hand when
she was small, then gave to her,
though black and tarnished by then,
when she left home to marry Jim.
Over the mantel, the oval photograph
of Granny Finney at thirteen, just before
she married Joe, then twenty-three.
The cross-stitched Quilter's Prayer
hanging on one of the bedroom walls:
*Dear Lord, make the bad people good*
*and the good people easy to live with.*

The little upstairs porch among the trees
in her front yard, panes so full of sun
and fields, a bird's-eye view of the road
below and all that passes by, where
she's made fifty quilts since Jim died,
where her guests down from Pennsylvania
sometimes sleep in two small beds
beneath windows opened to let in
the country air and night sounds.

Then to the cozy kitchen porch
flanked by two feathery Boston ferns
hanging gracefully from the eaves
and by rambling yellow tommy-toe
vines tied up to both the corner posts
with faded scraps of colored cloth.
Making the small talk usually meant
for Sunday afternoons, we name
trees in her yard, identify bird calls,
hear Emolene's home improvement
plans, the origin of the ruddy rhubarb
growing among the hostas at the edge
of the porch, and how the only way
to eat rhubarb pie is with plenty
of sugar, lots of thick, sweet cream.

Sitting forward in his rocking chair,
leaning over on his cane, George
stirs among the red potatoes,
the long green cucumbers
and yellow summer squash
he's gathered from his garden,
fetched along with a homegrown
watermelon, tokens, he laughs, required
before sister Emolene passes his plate.
Though she once solemnly observed,
*As long as my brother has anything to eat,*
*I know I'll always have something, too.*

As two jays fly to the black gum tree
and the hawk disappears from its perch
out back, a neighbor rides slowly by
in a two-wheeled cart drawn up the hill
with ease by a single chestnut mare.
No one thinks to check the time.

## Resurrection of a Primrose

*in memory of Katy Lee Finney*

What I have left to remember her by
is a small clump of yellow primrose
from her garden to mine, then transplanted
in a place with little room for growing anything.

The yardman must have thought it a weed,
cut it to the ground; I wept a hard wracking grief.
Carefully, I lifted its stub stem, its scraggly root,
tucked it elsewhere with little consolation.

Come spring, the earth breathed a waking sigh,
jostled the birds, roused the flowers and trees,
put heat into the hormones of small creatures,
then stretched into the longer light of the day.

From the scraggly root rose a stem, then a leaf,
then another, another stem, leaves, more stems
in a glorious resurrection like my affection for her
each time the yellow primroses explode in blooms.

## Roses Are Red

At the side door of the little
white clapboard house
on my grandfather's farm
where I grew up was a latticed
trellis, painted white, too,
woven with a climbing red rose.
On Mother's Day, we searched
for the prettiest ones, knocked
off the aphids, removed damaged
leaves, then pinned them on
our shoulders before church.
Red roses for mothers still living,
white for those deceased.
Our family of four all wore red
in those mid-century years.
Perhaps the tradition has faded,
but on this Mother's Day so late
in my own life, I marvel
I would still fix a red rose
above my heart. And I do,
if only in this little verse.

## All We Knew

*in memory of Henry "Buck" McCorkle*

*Ol' Man River* rolled up out of his throat
and through his dark lips like a stream
of gleaming golden marbles.
Tones as deep and velvety as his skin,
so resonant you could actually
feel the vibrations in your bones.

*Ol' Man River, that Ol' Man River ...*
as he scattered handfuls of green grit
on the worn wood floors of the two-story
brick schoolhouse where my momma, daddy,
all their brothers and sisters, and even
I learned to read, add and subtract.

*He must know somepin'* ... tending
the furnace which still burned coal
in the boiler room of the basement
where he gave out affectionate advice
and began the matchmaking
that would beget me and my two siblings.

... *but he don't say nothin'* ... packing
me into his old pick-up truck the days
my early maturity left me with blood
on my clothes, running down my legs,
cheerfully driving me the three miles home
without referring once to the reason.

*He just keeps rollin'* ... swabbing
his mop across the thick putrid glob
where some child lost his breakfast,
assuring, *Now don't you worry, honey.*
*Go on along. Ol' Buck will clean*
*this right up in no time.*

*...he keeps on rollin' along ...* giving me
that many-grains-of-sand-on-the-shore
advice as I poured out my sixth-grade
romantic distresses, he listened
with patience and earnest attention,
reassuring me there would be others.

*Ol' Man River, that ol' Man River*,
that's what he was to us, just rollin' along,
taking care of our school and generations
of little white children who felt safe
and loved under his warm watch, never
thinking his dark skin meant anything else.

## Tribute to a Grandmother

*in memory of my maternal grandmother*
*Ina Henkle Criddle Bost*

*That best portion of a man's life, his little, nameless,*
*unremembered acts of kindness and love.* -Wm. Wordsworth

Humble in her ways, devout in her beliefs,
slow and seldom to anger, quick to love
and forgive, long suffering in her sorrows.

Sees me through her kitchen window,
meets me at her back door, arms open,
her face alight with pure devotion.

Dries my tears with butter and syrup
on warm yeast bread, gently guides
my small childish woes quoting scripture.

Leads me to cherish family through their letters,
sifting through white dress boxes
of sepia photos telling me their stories.

Gives to me unhurried time, her patient ear,
her gracious presence, her softly spoken
words, her gentle smile, that tender touch.

Leaves me with memories, the warp and weft
threading the fabric of who I become,
of who I am more surely as my years pass.

I think of her often alone in that big house
with her AM radio, the birds for company,
wondering if she knows what she means to me.

*25 years on …*

I discover I sent her a love letter once, enclosed
a poem I wrote in tribute, that comes back to me
years later, found tucked in her Bible, treasured.

## Best I Could

*in memory of my father Paul Eugene Cansler*

Still mostly boy himself, more than handsome,
strong, and hard-working but burdened too much
with the cautious self-doubt of a shy country lad

most at home in the tall, long rows of green corn,
the wide waving ocher fields of wheat and oats,
the labors of pitching hay, silage, manure.

He knew how to erect a barbed-wire fence,
how to walk behind a mule and hand plow,
the secret call to bring cows with swollen udders

into the barn twice a day and which fingers,
manipulated just so, gave the pull of the teats
that brought warm strong streams of milk.

He learned to work for others, hold two jobs
at a time, buy a car and go to the bank in town
to borrow the money to build his own house,

four small rooms and a basement under roof,
his, and a shelter for those two little blond girls
he looked at with fear and so much fierce love.

Girls grow up, through stages, almost all trying
once they pass the giggling years of crawling
into their daddy's lap and laughing at his antics,

stages fraught with tempests of tantrums and terrors,
of tears and waves of hormones and histrionics
brushed with lush moments of unfolding wonder.

Given to few words, he never revealed his angst
beyond *did the best I could*, implying no doubt
*could have done better*, which, put into words ...

*if only I had known how, oh, how I wanted to give
you more, to lift you up to all that was in you, to be
your Protector, your Mentor, your Always Adored.*

But he knew how to love us simply and as surely
felt the burden of providing, the responsibility
of instilling his truths hoping we might honor them, too.

In the times I needed more, I turned elsewhere,
but I would always know he had done the best he could
just by wanting to be all the dad I'd ever need.

# Encounter at Aldi's Discount Grocery

*honoring my mother Carroll Bost Propst*

She pushes the cart aside
to give the cashier a hug,
a woman she doesn't know,
but familiarity's never a requirement.
*Do you need a hug? Had your hug today?*
she might ask, though permission
is never required either.
And might not always be granted
by those taken aback in her boldness
violating their personal space.

But at eighty-nine and filled
with so much joy it seems
she might burst if holding it in,
she sets her aim with confidence,
oblivious of propriety, blind
to any disruption, ignoring,
if she even notes it, discomfort.
Most, however, accommodate her,
some with glee, others with a slight blush
or a dazed expression as the moment sinks in.

Watching her, a small child speaks
as she passes leaning on her cane,
stopping to engage the youngster
with a gleefully animated smile.
Without hesitation, the little girl
steps toward her, arms reaching up
around the thick waist of the elderly
stranger for a hug of her own.
Who knows who is watching, receiving
even the smallest gifts we bestow,
or where a passing gesture might shine a light
in the shadows of somebody's longing?

## One More Memory

*for my daughter April Lynn Hawkins*

Along with the generous tip,
she takes her hairdresser
a snack each week ... cookies,
pack of crackers, an apple ...
often tucking her payment
in the small Ziploc bag
with the treat of the day.

Today, a slice of meat loaf
from her stash in the freezer.
Her granddaughter arrives,
asks if her grandmother has all
she needs to take with her.
*In the freezer*, her reply.

So it is, meat loaf carefully
wrapped in its own Ziploc, tucked
in another with thirty in bills.
Her granddaughter pauses, then
makes her grandmother laugh.

*Guess this time, Grandmama,*
*you will pay her in cold hard cash!*
Another memory tucked away
for later, as later comes sooner
than either of them will wish.

## Legacy of Remembrance

*for my sister Catherine (Kitty) Cansler DiNapoli*

Even after all these years,
you stay in touch with them,
classmates from high school, college,
some of your students gone on,
out and up remembering your
kindness, patience, encouragement.
A half century of your memories
with him, a home, a family, a life
archived in photos on every surface.
Pillows you made of Dad's shirts,
words of his love embroidered
on the pockets, a memento for
when our missing sets in again.
Now, you sew, shop, send cards
on every occasion, show up
for recitals, games, birthdays
to be part of every milestone
your grandchildren celebrate
so they'll know you're in their corner,
they in your spilling-over proud heart.
It's what you most want to leave them,
a trove of precious recollections
to hold in their hearts when you can
no longer hold them in your arms.

## The Recording

*for my brother Craig Paul Cansler*

Could that glorious explosion
    of sounds, that soaring sweep
of song filling the hall
        with raucous runs,
fitful chords, every nook
    and corner trembling
with energy, electric
    with awe, breathless
until the last note
                        echoing
    into the silence ...

    then broken
            at last
by rapturous applause
    going on
            and on,
    that small voice at the end
stunned, almost whispering,
        *Wow ...?*

Could that have been
    his hands flying
over the tiered console,
    left playing 7 notes,
the right, 5,
his feet dancing on four pedals,
    —all at once ...
then on in 32nd notes

to the next phrase,
no regular time
signature, only a practiced
beat, no melody
to lead the ear
—all memorized
in his fierce interpretation
of something close to the key of D,
so many accidentals
the key is hardly relevant?

Had he once played
this difficult piece in a master class
under the approving French composer?

Had he once brought Bach to rapture,
lured expression from clean voices
that seemed wrung from their souls?

Had those trained voices testified
to an experience so rich it could
not happen for them ever again?

Perhaps, it was him,
in some dreamy haze of life
long ago before he resigned
himself to another.
What was that about?

No desire to remember the bitter taste
of rejection he's tried to erase.

What of a return now years hence,
that old water long under the bridge,
new water stirring over the rocks,
frisky with light?

Can he feel the sweet taste
of possibility spreading
from his deep, deep down?

His body moves to the music,
one hand signals the beat,
one turns the pages.
He catches his breath,
forgetting I am there.

## Back to Before

When I retired I had to find
who I was now without a schedule,
no calling card to define me.
I rummaged about in the battered box
of memory, rifling through dog-eared
faded photographs of *Before*
until near the bottom I found myself
at twelve in blue jeans and a tee,
peacefully roaming my grandfather's farm
alone on a fine morning in mid-June.

There I was, if only I could
crawl back into that skin,
unknowing much of what I know now,
finding the tiny portal from doing
back into the being we dream
of when our working days are done,
feeling the red clay of the Catawba Valley
between my toes, in my bones
and caked all over my soul.

## Heritage

*Oh, John,* she exclaims
to her blind brother,
*I wish you could see her,*
of her grandniece dropped by
to visit while she is in town.
*She looks,* she goes on,
catching her breath,
*just like Mama!*
And shows the girl
the photo that sends
chills of recognition
into her young memory.
She understands now
she owes a debt to the past.

*My memories …*

# *Afterword*

## No Light Too Small

Everything goes bump
in the darkness of fear.
Fear knots the unknown
into long strands of what-ifs
that then grow of their own
terrified accord until their trail
disappears over the horizon
where the world we know ends.
Fear takes our breath, our tears,
clutches the heart in its fist,
seizes the brain in suffocating
tangled tentacles of despair.
Strike a match, light a candle.
Even if it goes out, you will have
seen enough to feed your dreams.

## About the Author

"Writing at this stage in my life offers me a perspective shaped by decades of experience. And hopefully, the maturity to temper that perspective with heart."

She grew up surrounded by her grandfather's farm and a large extended family in Catawba County, North Carolina. Her blue-collar parents made their livings in the shops and factories in that same county, dreaming of college for their kids.

Beverly C. Finney graduated from Mars Hill College, now University, set in the western part of her home state near Asheville, North Carolina. She double-majored in elementary education and English before completing her MA in English at Appalachian State University in Boone, North Carolina.

In her twelve years with Caldwell Community College and Technical Institute in Hudson, North Carolina, she established their first developmental English program, then gravitated to administrative work to eventually become the institution's first full-time public information officer.

That experience led to her 25 years with Blue Ridge Energy, a rural energy cooperative serving a five-county area in the Blue Ridge mountains and foothills. "Those co-op members, the deeply dedicated employees and the beauty of the area got in my blood. I left a good chunk of my heart there."

Now that she's retired, Beverly's work is writing. Her first collection, *Bearing Witness,* was published in 2019 by Third Lung Press (now Redhawk Publications) and is available on Amazon. "It's my way of 'bearing witness' to life, to living and to what I think it means to be "human" *Cracks in the Dark* continues that theme.

www.ingramcontent.com/pod-product-compliance
Lightning Source LLC
LaVergne TN
LVHW091007080826
845145LV00003B/1168

* 9 7 8 1 9 5 2 4 8 5 4 8 0 *